Praise for

JUST THREE MINUTES, PLEASE

"The intellect of a scholar, the s
professor of law: it hardly seen
embodied in one book of short t.

> — C. K. Williams, American poet, critic, and translator,
> and recipient of the Pulitzer Prize for Poetry

"*Just Three Minutes, Please* compiles Michael Blumenthal's pithy and insightful radio essays on life, politics, and the human condition. Engaging, astute, and eloquent, this book is a wonderful read."

> — Meenakshi Gigi Durham, bestselling author of *The Lolita Effect: The Media Sexualization of Young Girls and What We Can Do About It*

"David Sedaris and Ira Glass have a brother from another mother, and his name is Michael Blumenthal. His soulful NPR essays are profound thought-clouds from one of America's finest poets."

> — Dalton Delan, executive producer of "In Performance at the White House" for PBS

"Michael Blumenthal has had many professions—lawyer, psychotherapist, poet, professor, travel writer, novelist—and somehow these different professional perspectives blend together perfectly in his latest incarnation as a commentator for NPR. He writes with prickly piquancy and gleeful eclecticism on a broad range of topics—but is always, in the tradition of our best essayists, speaking from the baseline of his own humanity."

> — Ross McElwee, filmmaker and professor of Visual and Environmental Studies at Harvard University

"An enjoyable and liberating read."

> — Craig Manning, independent publisher

West Virginia University Press
Copyright 2014 Michael Blumenthal.
All rights reserved. First edition published 2014
by West Virginia University Press.
Printed in the United States of America

21 20 19 18 17 16 15 14   1 2 3 4 5 6 7 8 9

PB ISBN: 978-1-938228-77-3
EPUB ISBN: 978-1-938228-78-0
PDF ISBN: 978-1-938228-79-7

Library of Congress Cataloging-in-Publication Data:

Blumenthal, Michael. [Essays. Selections]
Just three minutes, please : thinking out loud on
public radio / Michael Blumenthal. First edition.

p.   cm

Consists of transcripts of the author's selected radio
broadcasts on West Virginia Public Radio.
ISBN-13: 978-1-938228-77-3 (pbk. : alk. paper)
ISBN-10: 1-938228-77-4 (pbk. : alk. paper)
ISBN-13: 978-1-938228-78-0 (epub)
ISBN-10: 1-938228-78-2 (epub)
[etc.]

I. West Virginia Public Broadcasting. II. Title.
PS3552.L849J87 2014
814'.54--dc23
2013035010

Cover Design: Michel Vrana
Book Design and Art Direction: Than Saffel
Author photograph: Judit Kepes

JUST THREE MINUTES,

Thinking Out Loud *on* Public Radio

PLEASE

Michael Blumenthal

VANDALIA PRESS
MORGANTOWN 2014

Think where man's glory most begins and ends,
and say my glory was I had such friends.

—*William Butler Yeats*

CONTENTS

INTRODUCTION

I have long felt that the brief essay is somehow the prose equivalent of the poem—yet one more effort to say as much as possible in the fewest possible words. No less a writer and philosopher than Friedrich Nietzsche once proclaimed it his ambition "to say in ten sentences what others say in a whole book," an ambition I believe poets and brief essayists share, without always achieving. When you are writing for the radio, not only word count but time itself are the two, often friendly, barriers you find yourself up against.

For me, who began as a poet and has wound up a law professor, the limits imposed by the brief radio essay—the idea of saying something both meaningful and lyrical in a scant 500 or so words—have provided some of the same liberations that most "prisons" of form impose, namely, the need to make every word count and to express every idea as succinctly and clearly as possible. As a poet and prose writer, I consider brevity as not only "the soul of wit," as

Shakespeare suggested, but also a kind of salve against boredom and repetition, a promise to leave the reader's good graces before we exhaust them.

"The hallmark of the personal essay," essayist and anthologist Phillip Lopate has written, "is its intimacy," and *that*, for this writer, has always been what drew me to the form, since intimacy—in both literature and life—is a quality I try to cultivate. To be sure, the brief essay, such as those included here, offers a different kind of intimacy than the ruminative, meandering essay in which Lopate (and, before him, Montaigne) specializes, and whose greater length both demands and allows.

But the radio essay—especially when it enters into the domains of politics, social policy, education, and the like— offers the special privilege of allowing its author to be both private and public at once . . . of allowing him to say something that, at one and the same time, is deeply personal to him and, yet, may also be of interest to a wider, more eclectic, public.

There is yet another view of the relation between the meandering and the brief, as reflected in the comment by the seventeenth-century French writer, philosopher, and inventor Blaise Pascal to the effect that, "I have only made this letter longer because I have not had the time to make it shorter." Pascal seemed to know something that the writer Stephen King also knows: that "brevity makes sweetness," or, at the very least, sweetness of a different kind. We live, for better or worse, in a world of limited patience and many alternatives upon which to exercise it, so at the very least it behooves someone lucky enough to have an audience not to bore them.

We might for example, remind ourselves that the most lyrical and profound public speech in American political discourse, Lincoln's *Gettysburg Address,* consisted of all of 272 words—a length that would have placed Lincoln well within the limits imposed by my genteel editors at West Virginia Public Radio.

All this is to say that what I've tried to do in these short pieces—in writing for both the eyes and the ears and given the liberty by my part-time colleagues to write about almost anything that moved me—is to create a kind of brief and catchy "prose poem," a species that, if it succeeds, will provide the listener/reader with some of the immediate pleasures of music, along with the more delayed gratifications of reflection.

As for what moves me, perhaps I should also say a few words about that, as mine has been—or so I am told—a rather unconventional career, along with an equally unconventional publishing history. I have written books of poetry, a novel, a memoir, a book of essays on Central Europe, a book about baboons in South Africa, and countless book and magazine articles about subjects ranging from cerebral asymmetry to slow virus diseases and tropical rainforests.

I am not, however, by any stretch of the imagination, a specialist on all of these subjects. I am, rather, an interested dilettante, a man with a sufficiently restless and unfocused intelligence to be interested in more things than one simple profession (aside from journalism) allows. In that realm, I take my cue from the great farmer, poet, essayist, and novelist Wendell Berry, who, in his marvelous book of essays, *The Unsettling of America: Culture and Agriculture,* wrote the following:

> It is suggested, both by the organization of the universities and by the kind of thinking they foster, that farming shall be the responsibility only of the college of agriculture, that law shall be in the sole charge of the professors of law, that morality shall be taken care of by the philosophy department, reading by the English department, and so on. The same, of course, is true of government, which has become another way of institutionalizing the same fragmentation.
>
> However, if we conceive of a culture as one body, which it is, we see that all of its disciplines are everybody's business, and that the proper university product is therefore not the whittled-down, isolated mentality of expertise, but a mind competent in all its concerns.

"A mind competent in all its concerns"—*that*, at least, is what I aspire to, surely without succeeding most of the time. A three-minute 500-odd-word essay is hardly, after all, the appropriate vehicle for displaying so Renaissance-like a competence. But it is, at the very least, a rather fine, albeit humble, vehicle for displaying a variety of *interests*, along with at least the hope that the brief needn't necessarily be equated with the superficial. And, incompetent as I may be in some of them, I am interested, and always have been, in *lots* of different things. Which may help to explain my somewhat schizophrenic-seeming career path and the varied duff and detritus of publications I have left in its wake.

But is there nothing, the reader might ask, that unites these essays beyond a kind of dilletantish interest in many things? I dare to say that there is, and to justify my claim I might borrow just a few more minutes of the reader's time to tell of an incident that took place in Paris in 2001. I was sitting in a café with the renowned Polish poet Adam Zagajewski, whose work I knew, but whom I had just met for the first time. "Why do you write?" I asked him, and he answered, without blinking an eye: "I write out of a search for meaning. . . . And why do *you* write?" he asked in turn. "I write," I answered with equal alacrity, "out of a craving for justice."

And that, dear reader, is my claim for the connection between these seemingly disparate pieces: They are all, or at least mostly, concerned with that craving for justice—be it in the personal, the political, or the public realm. They all strive—though I'm sure often without succeeding—to "hold in a single thought reality and justice," as the great Irish poet Yeats wrote that his mystical metaphors were intended to. And that too, for me, has been the intention here.

West Virginia—much like my other adopted home, Hungary—has proved a kind of inspiration to me, primarily because, like Hungary, it is so much more sophisticated and genteel a place than its reputation allows, and because

I have found within its borders both a refreshing variety of types and cultures and a kind of challenge to the clichés and stereotypes so many of us often think in.

Without the help and encouragement of Scott Finn, John Hingsbergen, Beth Vorhees and Ben Adducchio of West Virginia Public Radio, these essays would never have been birthed into existence, so I wish to thank them here, both publicly and sincerely. I also owe a debt of gratitude to the kind and helpful folks at West Virginia University Press—Carrie Mullen, Abby Freeland, Hillary Attfield, and Than Saffel.

My thanks also go out also to the many listeners who—whether in agreement or disagreement with the sentiments expressed in these pieces—were generous enough to make their reactions heard and to assure me, at least, that the major dread of every writer/essayist—the possibility that no one at all may be listening—had not, in my fortunate case, come to pass.

Morgantown, West Virginia
April, 2013

ACHES AND PAINS

THE UNKINDEST
CUT OF ALL

The knife enters you from behind, while you are fast asleep—or, rather, with your own consent, unconscious—having been guided into what the poet Robert Frost once referred to as "the dark of ether." It enters you, you imagine later, somehow cleanly and immaculately, held by what you have assumed to be the warm and capable hands of the one you have yielded yourself up to, like a penitent to a priest. But now, as the surgeon Richard Selzer has observed, there is no wine, no wafer. . . . The priest of this theater holds not a chalice, but a knife. And you are lying there, in this mock-death of yours, his meat.

When I was young and arrogant and, I was sometimes generously told, still relatively attractive, I always assumed that life's end would sneak up on me with a bold stroke—a heart attack on the tennis courts, a brain hemorrhage while making love . . . something quick, dramatic, and lyrical, like the death of the Metropolitan Opera's great baritone,

Leonard Warren, who fell lifeless onto the stage while intoning an aria from Verdi's *La Forza del Destino*.

Until several months ago, in fact, I had tended to think of myself, both physically and aesthetically, as a well-above-average sixty-year-old, someone whose good health, at the very least, consisted of what the English writer and entertainer Quentin Crisp once described as "having the same diseases as one's neighbors." I didn't, of course, actually *know* what diseases my neighbors had, but I consoled myself by assuming, that, at the very least, I was among the more fortunate.

But then, just a few weeks ago, and for the first time in my sexagenarian existence, came the surgeon's knife—a veritable knife in the back. "Surgeons must be very careful / When they take the knife," wrote the poet Emily Dickinson, [for] "Underneath their fine incisions / Stirs the Culprit—*Life*!" But, for me, it wasn't merely life that stirred beneath the surgeon's cut: it had been pain . . . months and months of unbearable, tear-wrenching pain from a deeply herniated disc—more tears, even, than failed love ever had brought . . . more tears, even, than thoughts of death. Nor did I want to accept without a fight Crisp's rather dour prediction that "the life of anyone who lives to be sixty *cannot* really have a happy ending, since the happy time is earlier than this." Maybe Crisp was right, but I, at least, was determined that there were some happy times still *ahead*.

The first surgery of one's lifetime is a kind of loss of virginity: There is, of course, the anticipation of relief and future pleasure, but it is commingled with uncertainty, dread and, yes, the fear of ineptitude as well. The contract between a patient and a surgeon—even in our modern age of relatively immaculate, high-tech incisions with names like Lumbar Micro Endoscopic Discectomy—is a special sort of agreement. "For the special congress into which patient and surgeon enter," Richard Selzer has written, "the one must have his senses deadened, the other his sensibilities restrained." Nor is it for no reason that the operating room is referred to as a "theatre." Within it, life and death, cure and failure—just as surely as in Hamlet or Macbeth—engage in their mortal combat.

"In a surgical operation," Selzer writes, "risk may flash into reality. The patient knows this too, in a direct and personal way, and he is afraid."

Afraid. That's indeed what I was: *afraid.* Waiting in the pre-op room, inhaling the antiseptic odors of God-and-the-doctors-only-knew-what, surrounded by men and women wearing H1N1-like masks, listening to the beeps, hums, and reverberations of machines I had no name for, I realized that, as Selzer puts it, I had made a declaration of surrender. It was not for sleep or love that I was allowing myself to be laid prone and various magical fluids injected into my body: It was for the sake of cure . . . for a second stab at being young.

A little more than an hour after relinquishing myself to the netherworld to which I had been escorted by a Greek anesthesiologist, I awoke from my drug-induced haze into the magical half-world of the recovery room, having to pinch myself twice to make sure I hadn't died. "In pain and nausea," Selzer has written, "you will know the exultation of death averted, of life restored." And if you are very lucky, as I was on this particular day, you might even gaze through the hazy mist of your now-more-mortal life—a bit older, a bit more tenuous, a bit wiser, you'd like to think—and see the face of someone you love: a merely human face, of course, but the kind of face that assures you it is worthwhile going on.

So you rise once more, an abbreviated phoenix. You are alive, but must now take your place firmly among life's wounded. "Life," as Quentin Crisp also put it, [is] "a funny thing that happened to me on the way to the grave."

You gaze up into your wife's kind and loving face. You will never, you know for certain, be the same again.

You are blessed.

November, 2009

THE QUALITY
OF OUR MERCY

I'm not the type of person who is supposed to be poster boy for the health care crisis. Not at all—I'm a law professor at West Virginia University, holder of two prestigious-sounding academic chairs, author of thirteen books, a man with a law degree from an Ivy League institution, and, once upon a time, a Harvard professor for a decade. None of this is to brag—it's just to provide a bit of context. Because people like me—almost anyone, particularly those in the health insurance industry, will tell you—aren't supposed to be uninsured, much less not even *provided* with health insurance by the institutions they serve.

But here I am, following four months of the most acute pain and suffering I've ever undergone, having just by the skin of my teeth avoided economic and physical disaster . . . and all this no thanks to the American health care system that, certain people argue, functions well and is in no need of change.

Here, in brief, is my story:

In my previous job, in which I held the lofty-sounding title of Mina Hohenberg Darden Endowed Chair of Creative Writing at Old Dominion University in Virginia, I was given—along with that distinguished-seeming honorific—the luxury of having *no benefits whatsoever*, health or otherwise. My home institution, in its infinite wisdom and largesse, seems to feel—as my previous employer, Harvard University, famously does—that prestige not only can be eaten, but can also pay the bills.

But let's leave Old Dominion—and its rather convenient excuse that an employee with less than a six-month contract (mine, conveniently enough, was written for five) cannot, by state law, be granted employee's benefits—at least for the moment, behind. Aside, that is, from mentioning that, bereft of health insurance provided by my former employer, I was forced—until last July 1st—to pay for my own health insurance under the COBRA plan that allows employees who have lost their insurance to retain the plan at their own expense for 18 months.

So . . . between last July 1st and last August 15th—when my employment at my far more generous and decent present employer, West Virginia University's College of Law, began—I found myself, for what I thought would be just a little over six weeks, among our nation's nearly 47 million uninsured.

Luck, of course, like health itself, can be a funny—or not

so funny—thing. And, as luck would have it, I found myself, on the to-me-unforgettable date of July 29th, screaming—no, virtually weeping—with pain, and, at my own expense, a patient in Budapest, Hungary's Rheumatological Institute. My stay there—including MRIs, spinal catheters and probes, round-the-clock nursing care and pain medications, all paid for by yours truly—lasted more than three weeks, forcing me to reschedule the reservation I had made to return to West Virginia on August 16th (believing, logically enough, that the onset of my health insurance coverage would coincide with the onset of my employment) for August 22nd. On that date, courtesy of wheelchairs and stretchers and a nearly $1,000 upgrade to first class, I returned to Morgantown.

But the health insurance industry, ever concerned with its coverees' welfare, had yet another surprise in store. For—although it seemed I was perfectly worthy of appearing at the Law School and resuming work as of the 15th—the very same human being who was good enough to teach and meet with students on that date wasn't quite yet "human" enough to insure. Instead, when I called the Benefits Office, I was politely informed that my benefits wouldn't "vest" until September 1st—two weeks after the beginning of my appointment!

The logic of this—surely the brainchild of the Public Employees Insurance Agency (P.E.I.A.), and, or so I like to think, not the University—is rather obvious: A person is only worthy of being insured once he or she had at least paid their "dues" by putting in two weeks' work. This, friends, is Darwinian capitalism in action: no return on your investment, no investment.

And so—from August 22nd until September 1st—I lay in my bed on the second floor of my house on Wagner Road, screaming with pain at every move, yet managing, somehow, to limp and be wheeled to teach my class, sometimes quite literally on my knees.

Nor was that quite the end of it. "You may also," I was alerted by a kind-hearted member of the Benefits Office staff, "fall under the exemption for pre-existing conditions." All of you listening, I'm sure, by now know what this means—quite simply put: no coverage.

Here, however, fortune momentarily smiled down upon me, for it turned out that—by a breath-baiting margin of two days—the expiration of my previous coverage had taken place only sixty, rather than the disqualifying sixty-two, days before the onset of my new insurance. Thus, by sheer luck, rather than thanks to the benevolence of the insurance industry, I found myself covered.

I, of course, am among the more fortunate of our 47 million-odd uninsured. The crack in our health care foundation that I fell into was merely a crack, not a bottomless pit. I am therefore *not* one of the hundreds of thousands who *have* been disqualified for a pre-existing condition, nor am I among the countless numbers driven into bankruptcy, poverty, homelessness, and—yes, even death—by lack of health insurance. All this, I needn't really add, in the richest country on the earth, and the one that most prides itself on its large-heartedness and generosity.

"No man is an island, entire of itself," the great poet John Donne famously wrote. "Every man is a piece of the continent, a part of the main . . . therefore never send to know for whom the bell tolls; it tolls for thee."

And now, in this great, big-hearted country we call America, it is tolling for us all. No insurance company studies or fear-mongering slogans can disguise this one unmistakable truth: It is time to insure us one and all, man, woman, and child, titled or untitled, employed or unemployed, educated or illiterate. For benevolence and large-heartedness tend to be simple and straightforward . . . only mean-spiritedness and selfishness require endless studies and confusing figures.

"The quality of mercy," as Shakespeare's Portia so eloquently tells us in *The Merchant of Venice*, "is not strain'd. It is an attribute of God himself." Nor should it be strained here, in this supposedly God-fearing country of ours. For only when mercy is voluntary—when it occasionally mitigates, or alters, the compulsions of the literal law—is it true mercy.

There should—now, finally, under a President who has made the passage of universal healthcare the benchmark of his ambitions—be no more cracks for people to fall into . . . not anyone, and not even blessed and lucky people like me.

May, 2012

SUM OF ITS PARTS

You don't need to be a genius, or a patient for that matter, to realize that there's something terribly wrong with the way medical services are delivered in this country, but it certainly helps to be the latter.

When I was a kid growing up in the ghettos of Upper Manhattan, we had a family doctor, Dr. Weissman, who came to our house with the quintessential black bag and treated my family for, among other things, my mother's cancer, my father's enlarged prostate, my grandmother's angina pectoris, and my own childhood asthma. Miraculously enough, he seemed to know about *all* these things and how to treat them, and did so, it now seems to me, with considerable success.

Flash forward some fifty-odd years and here I am in Morgantown, where, in the past three months, I have seen, not necessarily in that order, an ear, nose and throat specialist, a pulmonologist, a spinal surgeon, a gastroenterologist, and my family practice physician, though I'm not sure that's a complete list—all for the singular purpose of figuring out why I seem to have a persistent cough and scratching in my throat.

Along with this, I've had, or been ordered to have, the following tests: a chest x-ray, a sinus x-ray, a full blood work-up, a pulmonary function test, a total serum immunoglobin test, a soft tissue neck CAT scan with contrast, an abdomen and pelvis CAT scan with IV contrast, a gastroscopy, a fluoro Speech Evaluation Complex, a hypersens pulmonitis evaluation, an Epworth sleepiness exam, a polysomnography, and—the final indignity—a PH study, involving a plastic tube inserted up my nose and into my esophagus for 24 hours which, in a moment of rational self-pity, I decided to abort.

What all this has cost my insurance company and, by extension, those who, directly or indirectly, finance it, I'm not exactly sure, but I imagine that by now it must be approaching the GNP of some small nation. All this, at least thus far, without an accurate diagnosis, or a cure.

Let me say, lest it seem otherwise, that all of my many doctors seem like good, competent, well-intentioned people. One of them, at least, is a personal friend. But it also seems to me that, unlike Dr. Weissman's, their medical training must have consisted largely of three major courses: avoiding actual contact with the human body, writing prescriptions, and ordering tests.

Rarely, if ever, am I actually *touched* by one of these good people, and each of them—though they seem to know quite a bit about their particular area of the human anatomy— seem somewhat baffled by what to do about the whole. In fact, I sometimes feel a bit like a car owner who, with his or her car running badly, is sent to one mechanic to check the oil, another for the carburetor, a third for a tune-up, a fourth for cooling system, and so on: lots of people who know about parts, no one who knows about an entire car.

When I mentioned my frustration about this situation to my friend the pulmonologist, he merely shook his head sadly and replied "yes . . . and it's only going to get worse."

The body, I'm convinced, if not the spirit, must, in some purely physical sense, at least be equal to, if not greater than, the sum of its parts. But I'm just not sure these days that anyone still knows how to add them up . . . or even cares. And it seems to me no wonder that—when I look into the faces of the many specialists who probe and prescribe over the separate domains of my somewhat ailing anatomy— what I truly long to see is the long-gone face of good old Dr. Weissman.

June, 2012

VOTE WITH YOUR FEET!

Let me warn you at the outset: What I'm about to say is a kind of call to civil disobedience. So let me begin with the story of my last visit to a doctor's office—a visit I believe has become generic in this country of ours, with its highest medical costs and highest paid physicians in the world.

I arrived at the medical office ten minutes early for my 3:30 appointment, and—to be perfectly honest—had my name called by a nurse's assistant just a few minutes later, who then weighed me and ushered me into the usual small, windowless waiting room to check my blood pressure and question me about my medications. The doctor—or, rather, *a* doctor—would be with me shortly, she informed me, closing the door behind her and leaving me in what I have come to call the "*Waiting For Godot*" position. Some fifteen or twenty minutes later, an intern from *another* specialty arrived, and—after looking me over and asking me a series of questions similar to those already asked—told me that the *next* doctor would be in to see me soon, once again shutting the door behind her.

Flash forward another twenty minutes, and the door opened yet again, revealing, this time, not the doctor herself, but a medical resident, a cheerful and competent-seeming young man I'd seen before, who again looked me over, gave me some advice as to treating my condition, and—wonder of wonders!—again told me that "the doctor" would be with me shortly, closing the door to my little cubicle ever so gently behind him.

By now it was 4:45—a full hour and fifteen minutes past the time of my appointment—and—though I opened the door several times, both to let in some fresh air and scan the halls, the doctor herself was nowhere in sight. She was, I was told by a passing nurse, "running behind," and would be with me shortly.

As five o'clock rapidly approached, and with a few other things to accomplish before calling it a day, I decided to do what any self-respecting and educated consumer would do: I untied the little surgical robe I had been given, put on my street clothes, and walked out.

And that, dear listener, is exactly what I encourage *you* to do next time you are shunted from nurse's assistant to nurse to intern to resident and kept endlessly waiting in a cheerless, magazine-bereft little cubicle at *your* local doctor's office: *walk out.*

The truth is that the medical profession in this wealthy and wealth-producing country of ours is alone among the professions in assuming that *their* time is money, while *ours* is worthless. Not only are we treated, perhaps understandably enough, as guinea pigs for the training of interns and residents, but we are locked into a series of cheerless examination rooms waiting for each apprentice in turn, while our own hours—and with them, our work—can . . . well, do I really need to say it?

In Hungary, a former Communist backwater where I spend my summers, my dentist—someone who earns far less than our doctors here—schedules a full hour's appointment for every patient, sees each patient on time, and works with only one dental assistant—her mother. She, apparently, feels my time is as important as hers, which makes me wonder: Is it *truly* that impossible, in this great country of ours, to schedule medical appointments that even vaguely correspond to the time patients are actually seen?

It might be good, from time to time, to remind ourselves that we are *consumers* of medical services, *not* victims, that it is mere medical fiction that a doctor's time is priceless, while a patient's is expendable. And that we have the power to do the same thing consumers do everywhere—namely, to vote with our feet, right out our often unresponsive doctors' doors.

March, 2012

THE LAME OF
THE EARTH

The world is largely the domain of the healthy in body and spirit; it's not necessarily a fun place for the sickly and the lame. Neither of these are conditions I can claim to know *too* much about, but, in recent years, I have at least learned something of them: I've had three surgeries in three years since moving to West Virginia—on my back, my hip, and, now, on my right Achilles tendon—and have spent more time on crutches and in a wheelchair and assisted by a walker during that period than in all my previous life combined.

There's a big difference between a condition that is temporary and one that is permanent: For the former, at least, there's a light at the end of a tunnel, a harbinger of better times to come. Whether or not the philosopher Nietzsche was right about whatever doesn't kill us making us better, there isn't much we can't endure when we know our suffering will soon end. And suffering, at the very least, can deepen our humility and our capacity for empathy. For years now, I've admired the man who enters the WVU Student Rec Center alone with his walker every morning at the same time I do, removes his prosthetic leg, and lowers himself into the swimming pool beside me.

Now, I admire him even more.

For myself, these months I've spent in recent years seated in wheelchairs and making my way with walkers have taught me at least one thing: that it's not an easy life for the handicapped and lame. Among the first and most valuable things to go is one's independence. One finds oneself dependent, not merely on the kindness of strangers, but even more deeply on friends and loved ones. There's nothing like a few weeks in a wheelchair to teach you something about what the word "community" truly means.

"Your chance of rescue from any despair," wrote the late Reynolds Price, whom cancer of the spinal column left wheelchair-bound and without the use of most of his body, "lies, if it lies anywhere, in your eventual decision to abandon the deathwatch by the corpse of your old self and to search out a new inhabitable body."

This, it occurs to me, is exactly what the permanently lamed and handicapped must learn to do: abandon the deathwatch by the corpse of their old selves and search out a new inhabitable body, a body which, while it may no longer be all they wished for, can still be the locus of pleasure and joy. But, if my weeks and months of immobility and dependence have taught me anything, they have taught me this: *it isn't easy.*

The handicapped—despite a world that has grown progressively more aware of, and amenable to, their existence—have their work cut out for them in human structures not designed with them in mind. Steps, hills, curbs, stones, uneven pavement, and inclement weather are but a few of the daily challenges they face . . . not to mention keeping their spirits up and simply making it to work. Just try making your way, as I tried to do unsuccessfully just a few days ago, into the new Sweet Frog Yogurt Shop in Morgantown's Granville Mall in a wheelchair, for example, and you'll see what I mean. It's not only not easy—*it's impossible*. In the world we know, despite the title of Flannery O'Connor's famous short story "The Lame Shall Enter First," the intact of body have, no pun intended, a real leg up.

For myself, my blessedly temporary sojourns among the lame and the handicapped have forced me to take on a new kind of alter-ego: no longer as dependent on my physical prowess and agility, and more dependent on my own, less outwardly obvious but at least equally useful, inner resources. My steps may have grown slower, but my gazes into the magnificent and often-ignored outer world that surrounds me have grown longer and more penetrating. The eternal interchange that life forces us to make between the demands of the soul and the capacities of the body has, like the earth's tectonic plates, shifted . . . and not necessarily for the worse.

I've been among the handicapped only a short time, and—lucky me—I assume only temporarily. But it's been enough to teach me something of what they, on a daily basis and often for the rest of their lives, must endure. They may not need our sympathy, but of one thing I'm entirely certain: they most surely deserve our admiration.

July, 2012

ALMOST HEAVEN

THE WILD, NOT-SO-WONDERFUL
WHITES OF WEST VIRGINIA

The several generations of the White family of Boone Country, West Virginia depicted in the recent documentary covering a year in their lives *are* most certainly white—and there is hardly anyone who would dispute the fact that they are wild. The question of whether or not they are, as the film's tongue-in-cheek title suggests, also wonderful, or whether they are, somehow, representative of West Virginians, however, is, to say the least, open to dispute.

West Virginians, let's face it, suffer from what many Americans, and even those in my two other part-time countries, France and Hungary, might call a bad name. Even former Vice President Cheney found some tasteless way to mock West Virginians, and jokes like

What do a tornado and a West Virginia divorce have in common?
Answer: Someone always loses a trailer.

or

Why did O. J. Simpson want to move to West Virginia?
Answer: Because he heard that everyone has the same DNA.

not only exist, but abound. And if the jokes aren't enough, our great state is also referred to by novelist Jonathan Franzen, in his new smash bestseller *Freedom*, as "the nation's own banana republic, its Congo, its Guyana, its Honduras."

For those already predisposed to generalizing negatively about the citizens of this beautiful state, *The Wild and Wonderful Whites of West Virginia* will hardly do much to help our cause. The members of this legendary family, depicted here in all their dubious glory and glorious lack of modesty and shame, drink to excess, snort coke while still hospitalized after the birth of their children, shoot each other in the faces, get killed, rob, propagate indiscriminately, and, when crime finally ceases to pay, even sing and tap dance . . . and pretty well at that. They suffer from, or enjoy, depending on your viewpoint, what the late novelist William Styron called "anarchic individualism." To put it simply, these are not the kind of folks you want your kids to marry . . . or even, if such a thing were remotely possible, have a single beer with.

I myself grew up on the tiny East Coast island of Manhattan, but I've always, for some reason, *loved* West Virginia and West Virginians. Back in the 70s and 80s, while living and working in D.C., I spent almost every free fall and spring weekend in one of West Virginia's magnificent state parks; paddled (or was paddled) down the white waters of the Cheat, the Gauley, and the New; bathed in the revivifying waters of Berkeley Springs and, when I felt particularly flush, the Greenbrier; and I got to know—and *like*—West Virginians as a people, admiring their fierce and independent spirit and their willingness to be, unapologetically, who they were.

That, indeed—their independent spirit—may be something to admire even about the Whites, who, if nothing else, aren't ashamed of who they are, though some might argue they ought to be. *Are they an attractive role model for our children?* Hell, no. But they are, at the very least, real . . . very real indeed.

Since moving to Morgantown—a town, I well realize, that is hardly representative of the state—my affections for West Virginia have not only been confirmed, but deepened. And my sphere of reference isn't confined to my students and colleagues at the College of Law, or to the University community in general. It includes my mechanic, my plumber, my neighbors, some of the homeless people I've talked to on the street, and most of those I've met on my travels throughout the state.

The salient fact I want to argue here is that, statistics and stereotypes be damned, the Whites are no more representative of West Virginia than Florida pastor Terry Jones is representative of the Christian citizens of Gainesville, or the terrorists who flew into the World Trade Towers are representative of Muslims, or the three unemployed drunks at the bar in my tiny Hungarian village are representative of Hungarians. Nor are they any more representative than two of West Virginia's more *positively* renowned citizens, the writer and Afro-American scholar Henry Louis Gates, Jr., born in Mineral County's county seat, Keyser, and the novelist Jayne Anne Phillips, born in Buckhannon.

People are only people—as individuals, families, clans, races, religions, and communities—and the more quickly we stop generalizing about who, and what, they are, the more quickly we will learn to live in peace and acceptance with one another. The Whites of Boone County may be wild indeed and not the kind of people most of us would like to have for neighbors. But there *is*, nonetheless, I would suggest, something wonderful about them—if for no other reason that they remind us that every one of our categories is, in truth, a cornucopia, that each of us, is one of a kind . . . no matter what kind that may be.

September, 2010

TALE OF TWO COUNTRIES

An old friend of mine, the former U.S. Poet Laureate Howard Nemerov, once said that when two things are said to have nothing in common, it is the duty of intelligence to show how alike they are. The same, I would argue, goes for places. And so, though I'm some 5,000 miles from West Virginia, in the small village of Hegymagas, Hungary, near the shores of Lake Balaton, as I write this, it's West Virginia I'm thinking of. For I've come to find my two adopted homes, though perhaps never before spoken of in the same breath—much less the same essay—strangely alike.

For one, both of these land-locked provinces, West Virginia and Hungary are, at least in the popular imagination, adamantly unglamorous places. In Europe and America alike, it's fashionable to malign my two homes and their citizens. Magyars, not unlike Mountaineers, are said to be fat, alcoholic, unhealthy, chain smokers, serial divorcers, and enthusiastic committers of suicide. The Jamie Olivers of the world, I'm sure, would have at least as much fun amusing themselves over a typical Hungarian breakfast as about the contents of a rural West Virginian freezer. A Hungarian version of *The Wild and Wonderful Whites of West Virginia*, for that matter, might easily be called *The Wild and Wonderful Kovaces of Kaptalantoti*.

Yet I love both places, and have come to consider them, in a spiritual and physical sense, home.

Why? you might ask. Most of all, because of this very unglamorousness: Unlike being from Paris or Aspen or San Francisco or Venice, no one has ever gotten any bonus points for being a Hungarian, *or* a West Virginian. There's nothing fashionable about being from Morgantown, or my tiny little Hegymagas—but there's something solid, deeply earthbound, about being from either. In both places, whatever you are, or may yet become, is something you will have *earned*. You'll never find, in boldface, on anybody's resumé: Birthplace: Hungary, or Birthplace: West Virginia, though you *may* find the occasional chicken paprika or ramps with bacon and hard-boiled eggs on some out-of-the-way restauranteur's eclectic menu.

There are many other qualities that residents of my two homes share, among them a low tolerance for what, in polite circles, is called "BS." If you say to a Hungarian, in coded New Yorkese, "let's have lunch sometime," the immediate reply is: "*When?*" West Virginians too, I've found, tend to say what they mean, and mean what they say, though it's not always what you want to hear. In West Virginia, as in

Hungary, charm can get you in the door, but it won't get you very far once you're in the house.

So I love Hungary and West Virginia, quite simply, because they are what they are, and neither expends much energy pretending otherwise. And both these soft-spoken places, from within the borders of their modesty, have produced exceptional scholars, artists, musicians, scientists, athletes, and song. What would the history of American politics have been, for example, without Robert Byrd? Or the world of music without Franz Liszt?

By the time you hear this, of course, I will be sitting in the WVPM studios in Morgantown again, speaking into a microphone. But, strangely enough, even as I sit here now, there's a big part of me that still feels that it might as well be Hungary. And, next time I'm in Hungary, I have a feeling it will feel a helluva lot like West Virginia.

September, 2011

VOTING, IN
BLACK AND WHITE

I am usually rather proud to be a naturalized West Virginian—proud because I've found the citizens of this state to be decent, friendly, intelligent people, far removed from the stereotype much of our nation has of them.

But, lately, I'm not quite so sure. Some weeks ago, more than 42 percent of my fellow West Virginians voting in our state's Democratic Primary, some 42,490 individuals, cast their ballots for a man named Keith Russell Judd—also known as Inmate No. 11593-051 at the Federal Correctional Institution in Texarkana, Texas, where he's doing time for extortion and threats made in 1999. Judd got on our state's ballot, along with those of several other states, simply by paying a $2,500 fee and filing a form known as a notarized certification of announcement.

One of West Virginia's two Democratic senators, Joe Manchin, along with our Democratic governor, Earl Ray Tomblin, wouldn't even *say* who they voted for in the primary, but, no matter how you cut it, the implication of this vote seems rather clear: Over 40,000 Democratic citizens of this state would prefer a convicted felon who doesn't even *live* here to what may be the best educated, most articulate, and most thoughtful President we've had in the last century.

"Keith Judd's performance is embarrassing for Obama and our great state," outgoing West Virginia GOP Chairman Mike Stuart said, arguably reflecting the first time I've agreed with anything a West Virginia Republican has said since moving to our great state over three years ago: embarrassing indeed. Mr. Stuart is right: It's enough, methinks, to make a reasonable person pause and rethink their loyalties.

It's no secret, of course, that President Obama's energy policies and the Environmental Protection Agency's handling of mining-related permits have incurred the wrath of West Virginia's coal industry, the second largest in our nation, and of other West Virginians as well. Given this fact, a simple question suggests itself: If you are so opposed to Obama, why not do the obvious thing, and simply vote for Romney?

But I can't help thinking there's a far uglier subtext to our Democratic primary vote—namely, race. However you analyze the motives behind Judd's 40,000-plus votes, one fact is patently clear: Judd is White; our President is, at the very least, half Black. I'm not a betting man by nature, but I'm eagerly willing to bet that had the convicted out-of-state felon running against President Obama been a Black man the result would have been radically different.

There are only fifteen states with a lower percentage of Black population than West Virginia, and I'm far from willing to agree with the stereotype that ours is a racist state. We have Black judges and Black legislators, I have Black colleagues at the College of Law and we have an increasing percentage of Black lawyers and Black law students. Most of the good people I know in this state are neither racist nor prejudiced, beyond the prejudices that lurk even in the best of us. But the fact remains that there is something deeply disturbing about a state in which more than 40 percent of its Democratic voters prefer a White felon to a Black president.

"I'm not voting for somebody who's in prison," a certain West Virginia electrician who claimed to be a conservative Democrat, told the Associated Press. This voter—one I am fairly sure is not entirely unrepresentative of some other West Virginians—seemed certain of one thing:

"I just want," she added, "to vote against Barack Obama."

May, 2012

FOUL PLAY!

To say something less than unconditionally positive about football in West Virginia is a bit like badmouthing the Holy Trinity at the Vatican. But what else are essayists for than to stir up a little trouble?

So I'll begin with some rather obvious principles that even football fans might agree with:

1. The most important thing that should go on in a university is what goes on in its classrooms, not on the football field.

2. By extension, the most important *people* at a university are its students and professors, *not* the football coach.

3. No football coach in America, be he professional or collegiate, is worth—as, for example, the head coach at the University of Alabama, Nick Saban, is paid—fifteen times the salary of the President of theUnited States, or, perhaps a bit less sensationally, some eighty times the salary of the average Shakespeare scholar.

In the capitalist system of which we are a part, what we pay for things, inevitably, is a reflection of the value we place upon them, so that the above statistics—to which I might add the fact that WVU Coach Dana Holgorsen makes some sixty-six times the annual salary of the Chief Justice of the United States and the *average* annual pay for a head coach in Division I NCAA football in 2009 was $1.36 million—must say something about our values as a community, *and* as a nation. If Texas Governor and presidential candidate Rick Perry truly thinks Congressmen are overpaid, I can only imagine what he thinks about the salaries of our college football coaches.

Now, before you turn off your radio and dismiss this writer as just another transplanted nerd from New York City, let me say that I've actually come to *like* football, and have become a fan, since moving to West Virginia. I enjoy spending the occasional invigorating fall Saturday among 60,000 cheering fans at Milan Puskar Stadium. I also think there are many positive things college football does for a school, a community, even for families themselves, and for this beautiful state.

But what I'm talking about here is not a matter of being for or against football. It's rather a matter of wanting, somehow, our system of rewards and attention to be in sync with our values, of wanting our universities to be intellectual breeding grounds first, and playgrounds, if at all, a distant second. The question of the relationship between academic life and college athletics is not, methinks, one of either/or, but of *how*. For a university, in the best sense of the word, is not merely about the intellect, or even the spirit, but about the body as well, and ought to do its best to foster a healthy relationship between the three.

"The culture of football in American universities," Steven Salzberg recently wrote in *Forbes* Magazine, "is undermining our education system and hurting our competitiveness in technology, science, and engineering. If we keep it up, the U.S. will eventually be little more than the big, dumb jock on the world stage—good for entertainment on the weekend, but not taken seriously otherwise."

Mr. Salzberg is right. Students come to this country, and to WVU, from all over the globe because of our universities' reputations as the best in the world. And we owe it to them, and to ourselves, to make sure that what they leave with—as former University of Chicago President Robert Maynard Hutchins (whose great university is referred to in at least one college catalog as "the place where fun goes to die") suggested—is "an onionskin with which to transform their intellectual nakedness," not merely a pigskin on which to inscribe their academic indifference.

December, 2011

COUNTRY OF THE SECOND CHANCE

UNWIRED

I have a very reliable friend in the world of cyberspace. It's called the "delete" button, and I make use of its generosities at least several times a day. Using it, I can remove from my fields of vision and consciousness not only the myriad junk mails offering me greater sexual satisfaction and time shares to destinations I have no desire to visit, but also memberships in what—with increasing Orwellian fervor—are described as the "social technologies," a pairing of words I consider as much of an oxymoron as some of my friends consider "academic life."

Recently I was treated, on the Charlie Rose show, to an interview with a charming, bright-eyed, and attractive young woman by the name of Gina Bianchini, the CEO of yet another new "social technology" called Ning. Ning specializes, its energetic creator tells us, in "creating and discovering social networks for your interests and passions." This, in addition to its 465 million dollars worth of corporate value, apparently distinguishes Ning from such other social technologies as Facebook, which allows us to connect with those we already know (a redundancy I can't, for all my best efforts, quite comprehend), LinkedIn, which allows us to maintain and develop "professional connections" (a reality I understand all too well), and Twitter, which enables us to communicate about new and real-time (as opposed, I imagine, to false-time) events.

"We actually want to be in different places for different things," Ms. Bianchini explains in her interview, "and to separate out of social identities into different places for different reasons." The mechanism for this, she continues, using a phrase that, to my mind at least, evokes more of sunburn and disease than passion and friendship, is, in her words "people peeling off" to create new networks in "viral loops."

"The really important thing," Ning's founder concludes, "is that people are voting with their time," creating such new Ning networks as, to name but a few, the Eastern Washington Powder Church for Northwest Powder Skiers, Firefighter Nation, Mugglespace, and Ryan & Sean's Not So Excellent Adventures.

But I, too, am "voting with my time"—which is to say that I am voting, with a happy squeeze of my right pinky, to keep my space precisely what it is . . . my space, not yours. Having now spent sixty-odd years finding, and choosing, friends in the time-honored, old fashioned way—that is, by *meeting* and *selecting* them in real time, real space, and real ways—I have no desire whatsoever to have strangers writing on my walls, to be "friended" by those I hardly even want as acquaintances, to be linked up to more people than I am already entwined with, or to share my passions with a network of any sort.

This will, I am quite certain, make me sound like something of a Neanderthal, but I still consider a "network" something I turn to on my television, a "technology" something I use to *escape* from my fellow humans (rather than to find them), and a "friend" as someone I have actually met, and *chosen* to invite into what I still happily consider my small and selective little universe.

All this may, indeed, leave me as an outsider to the brave new world of "social technologies," but it leaves me, happily, with friends I can see and touch, passions I can enjoy in private, and a delete button with which—by merely the touch of a finger—I can save myself from having to choose from a menu in a restaurant I never freely wandered into, and from whose choices there's nothing—*nothing at all*—I have any desire to eat.

May, 2012

COUNTRY OF THE SECOND CHANCE

There are two alternative versions of America, it has sometimes occurred to me, and they begin, as you approach my age, to offer radically different outcomes. The first was proposed by the writer F. Scott Fitzgerald, creator of that mythic American anti-hero Jay Gatsby, some seventy years ago. "There are," Fitzgerald wrote in his notebooks, "no second acts in American lives." And for Fitzgerald, dead at the age of forty-one by way of drink and dissipation, indeed there weren't.

But there's also a second vision of America, one which I myself prefer and which, if you drink a bit less than Fitzgerald did and get at least eight hours of sleep, you may yet come to appreciate. And that is that America is also the country of the second, and sometimes, even, the third and fourth chance. That, rather obviously, is a far more consoling, and, I believe, far truer, vision of our country than Fitzgerald's, and it may, I would suggest, even serve you in good stead as you contemplate, or dread, your own future.

I was a law student and a lawyer once—a smart, combative, argumentative and, I have no doubt, rather annoying law student—who, for many of the same neurotic reasons I am currently teaching law students about in my *Psychology for Lawyers* class at WVU, "bailed out" of the legal profession rather early and went on to a not entirely unsuccessful career as a writer. That's a trajectory, I know, that might be the envy of many of those now practicing law and who are champing at the bit to get out to what they envision as greener, or at least more glorified, pastures. Nor am I complaining about my fate.

Quite on the contrary, I'm here to celebrate it.

The fact is that, despite my love of writing and literature, the law and its intellectual, real-world allure never quite left me: I continued to dream of law school and lawyering, it seemed to me, almost nightly and, while still in the to-many-people enviable position of being Director of Creative Writing at Harvard, even went to see the Federal District Judge in New Hampshire who had offered me a clerkship fifteen years earlier to ask him if he might consider doing so again.

Which he did.

And I—still perverse and confused to the core—turned him down once more.

But now it's many years later, and by way of one of those propinquitous quirks and detours that makes America a kind of psychological nirvana for those who want to re-invent, or re-imagine, themselves, I find myself, of all things, *a law professor* . . . and a happy one at that. The fact is, I *adore* my colleagues and students at The College of Law. I find teaching and thinking about the law at least as inspiring as reading the poems of eighteen-year-olds, and—full disclosure—even relish the somewhat more substantial paycheck my efforts are met with.

So what I've found is that—despite the more frequent aches and pains it entails, and the occasional chemically induced assistance it may require with your love life—growing older, if you can manage to hang on long enough, not only gives you a second chance: it teaches you humility.

What you once detested, you may even find, should longevity bless you, you may yet grow to love; what you once avoided like the plague may yet prove the cure for many of your ills.

Though I am hardly an unquestioning American patriot—*au contraire*, as the French would say—I cannot also fail to acknowledge that it was this country, when my parents and my entire family were at the door of Nazi Germany's ovens, that gave *them* a second chance . . . and that it's also given one to me.

This may not sound like patriotism to some, but it has, at least, the virtue of truth. And it's a truth that, if you're lucky and long-lived, not only won't bang a door shut in your face, but, you may yet find, will even open some windows.

May, 2010

IMMIGRATION NATION

Should you aspire to being a demagogue in contemporary America, or simply a panderer, or an ordinary politician, there may be no single better issue onto which to hang your ideological hat than immigration. Immigration, as a recent article observed about Florida Senator Marco Rubio, can be a super-politician's "kryptonite"; it can also be his or her ticket to prominence and power.

We are *all*, of course, children of immigrants—whether our ancestors came over on the Mayflower or crossed the border beneath a barbed wire fence from Mexico—a fact highlighted by comedian Pat Paulsen's remark that "All the problems we face in the United States today can be traced to an unenlightened immigration policy on the part of the American Indian." But that collectively shared fate does little to dampen the thoughtless hysteria surrounding the immigration issue, or the zeal of those who, in an economically precarious time, would fan the fires of our fears. Giving us your tired, your poor and your huddled masses yearning to be free may sound just fine as a slogan engraved on the Statue of Liberty: In practice, however, it meets with far less than universal appeal.

No less moderate a politician than Lyndon Johnson once commented that "our land flourished because it was fed from so many sources—because it was nourished by so many cultures and traditions and peoples." And the truth is that immigrants often tend to be more American than people born here.

Sound bites notwithstanding, the immigration issue is complex, and not amenable to easy answers or facile slogans. Within its purview are contained some of our most conflicting emotions—the wish for universal justice and fairness, the desire for personal and economic security, our general fear of all that is alien, the desire to maintain our privileged status in the world, and a widely shared feeling that a nation should first take care of its "own," howsoever that "own" may be defined.

Some of my friends have argued, not unpersuasively, that, given the obvious injustices of what country and family sheer luck has us born into, people should be allowed to live, and obtain citizenship, in any country they can manage to get to. In a more perfect universe, that might be a justified conclusion, if only human nature and economic insecurity didn't keep getting in the way.

What the immigration issue requires, in fact, is a deeply honest and deeply probing inquiry into what we as a people are, a fundamental re-examination of our notions of justice and citizenship, of fairness and well-being. Like most complex political issues, it can't be solved by mouthing platitudes about freedom, or the land of opportunity, or by deluding ourselves about the genuine insecurities and ungenerosities within our nature. Much as we covet and politically reward simple answers to complex questions, immigration is one question that defies such simplifications.

Solving it, or even coming up with a compromise, is no easy task, to be certain. It will require, as do most issues of justice, determinations made *both* in abstract generalizations and individually, on a case-by-case basis. And arriving at a consensus about those questions may be almost as difficult as being human.

January, 2012

SOME TRULY AFFIRMATIVE ACTION: A FARMER ON THE SUPREME COURT

My College of Law faculty colleague, Jim Elkins, came over the other day with a novel idea. "What we *really* need on the Supreme Court," Jim said, "is a farmer."

Both Jim and I are the offspring of farmers he of generations of farmers who farmed and raised cattle on the fertile lands of far western Kentucky; I of immigrants who merely raised egg-laying chickens in southern New Jersey. But both our ancestors shared a certain earthbound wisdom: They knew what it was like to honor the rhythms of nature; they knew what it was like to be dependent, not on the money *money* can make, but on the money labor deserves. Above all, they were people dependent not entirely on their intellects, but on two more and more endangered commodities—practicality and common sense.

Because the practical is almost always the enemy of the ideological, a farmer on the Supreme Court would, by definition, cut across ideological lines. His or her conservatism would be a conservatism of the deepest kind: one that seeks to *conserve* the values of this only earth we will have a chance to inhabit. At a time when at least several of the hundreds of cases that will emanate from the recent disasters in the West Virginia mines and the fisheries of the Gulf will no doubt end up being decided by the Supreme Court, what better kind of person to have sitting there than one who will interpret the law with an ultimate loyalty, not just to the Constitution, but to the planet itself?

Solicitor General Elena Kagan, President Obama's not unsafe choice to fill the current vacancy on the Court, will, in all likelihood, soon be confirmed, followed by a swift round of self-congratulation at the Court's now having, for the first time in its history, three female justices, two Jews, an African-American, a Hispanic-American, and *even* three non-Harvard Law School graduates, who merely condescended to go to Yale.

This, however, will still leave unrepresented most of the constituencies that truly make up our national fabric— mid-Westerners and West Virginia University College of Law graduates, to name but a few. But most glaring among them would be to add one of America's historically most representative citizens—a farmer—to our nation's highest bench.

"Intellectuals solve problems," wrote one of our greatest, Albert Einstein, "geniuses prevent them." Thomas Jefferson, who knew a little something about *both* farming *and* government, felt likewise. "Agriculture," he wrote in a 1787 letter to George Washington, "is our wisest pursuit, because it will in the end contribute most to real wealth, good morals, and happiness."

So, at this juncture in our history, when we could well use a little more real wealth, good morals, and happiness, a farmer on the Supreme Court might just be a first step toward curing our ills. Such an appointment—President Obama's *next*—would indicate that we are a country committed not only to the life of the mind, but to the needs of the earth, not only to those who can reap and sow with their intellects, but who can harvest with their hands. By doing so, the President would be doing something the French writer Marcel Proust claimed intellectuals are virtually incapable of:

He would show himself capable of saying a simple thing in a simple way.

June, 2010

THE BUSINESS OF AMERICA

Former Massachusetts Governor Mitt Romney would like—how's that for an understatement?—to be President of the United States. He enthusiastically holds forth, as his chief qualification for doing so, his previous success as a millionaire businessman. The oracle at which Romney and his devotees worship is rooted in the words of America's thirtieth President, Calvin Coolidge, who, in a speech given before the American Society of Newspaper Editors in Washington, D.C., on January 17th, 1925, famously proclaimed that "the chief business of the American people is business," a proposition Romney and his supporters wholeheartedly defend.

Those words, however, are all the Republican frontrunner seems ever to have read of Coolidge's speech that day. But the then-President went on to conclude with some rather more profound sentiments. "Of course the accumulation of wealth cannot be justified as the chief end of existence," he continued. "We make no concealment of the fact that we want wealth, but there are many other things that we want very much more. We want peace and honor, and that charity which is so strong an element of all civilization.

"The chief ideal of the American people," Coolidge concluded, "is idealism. I cannot repeat too often that America is a nation of idealists. That is the only motive to which they ever give any strong and lasting reaction."

Let's hear it for dear old Calvin! *Peace, honor, charity, idealism*—words one doesn't often hear from the lips of Romney—or, for that matter, any of the *other* now-fallen Republican candidates either. But those are the words that characterized the America *my* parents, refugees from the horrors of Nazi Germany, embarked onto in June of 1938. They, too, wanted to make a good living here, and, from the point of view of relatively modest middle-class standards, they did. They wanted the opportunity, security, freedom, and ability to succeed through hard work that America has always stood for. But it never occurred to them, nor has it to me, that the true business of America is business.

Business, indeed, as the core of Coolidge's much-misunderstood speech suggested, is what has made a great deal of America's *other* successes possible. It has provided many Americans with economic well-being, a sense of security, and the ability to provide jobs for and consider the needs and misfortunes of others. But these seem to be essentially American qualities both Romney and his fellow business worshippers often miss.

"The American people are the greatest people in the

world," the putative Republican candidate has said on at least one occasion. "What makes America the greatest nation in the world is the heart of the American people: hardworking, innovative, risk-taking, God-loving, family-oriented American people."

But what about the qualities *I* love most about Americans and want in my President? What about compassion, large-heartedness, generosity of spirit, a respect for personal freedom, a willingness to share our abundance with those who have so little? Why are *those* qualities nowhere on our multi-million dollar candidate's lips? Why did he apparently never *finish* reading Calvin Coolidge's wise and measured speech?

Personally, I prefer having a President who's rich in spirit to one who's rich in investments. I prefer having a President who believes that one of the most significant businesses of America, once we have enough to care for ourselves and our families, is helping those less fortunate than we are. I prefer having a President who believes that Trayvon Martin could have been his own son to one who believes the Trayvon Martins of the world are alien beings on whom we should turn our backs, or draw our guns, out of fear that they might threaten our complacency and reinforce our prejudices.

In other words, I much prefer the President we've already got.

May, 2012

BP AND OUR
HUMAN SHADOW

The Swiss psychologist Carl Gustav Jung famously invented the term "shadow" to describe the way we humans divorce ourselves from our darker impulses and project them out onto others, in whom they are far safer and less threatening for us to despise than in ourselves. In Jung's eyes, at least, all forms of hatred were suspect, since he felt they usually involved some sort of *self*-hatred projected out onto others.

The latest victim of this tricky human habit of projection, I would suggest, is none other than BP CEO Tony Hayward, a man (and a company) I myself have no great affection for, but who I nonetheless feel is getting a kind of psychological raw deal in our frenzy to find a "villain" for our and society's misdeeds, and, therefore, not to have to deal with them ourselves.

Tony Hayward, in case you haven't noticed, seems able to do nothing right in the two-plus months since the Gulf oil spill disaster first took place. His apologies lack sincerity, his wish to "have my life back," seems callous, his taking a single day off from this ongoing tragedy to attend a yacht race is described as reflecting "gall" and "arrogance," and he has been dragged before several committees of our Congress, whose members seem to find no loftier platform for their own self-aggrandizement than belittling, insulting, chastising him, and calling for his resignation.

Let me get this straight: I *detest* the oil companies and their greed, I *abhor* their prioritizing profits over human safety, I am no great fan of Tony Hayward's to say the least, and I feel that BP should pay for every penny of the damage they have caused and the lives they have derailed and ruined. But that's an entirely other matter. For I also believe that "The fault, dear Brutus," to quote Cassius in Shakespeare's great play, *Julius Caesar*, "is not in our stars, but in ourselves that we are underlings."

And underlings we indeed are: underlings to an economy of waste and excess indulgence in, and demand for, fossil fuels; underlings to needs we are told we have but do not, in fact, have; underlings to an unsustainable level of demand for the products that companies like BP then drill for and market to us at our own peril.

For myself, at least, there is something eerily similar in all this to the Enron scandal, where we decided that Kenneth Lay and Jeffrey Skilling were the incarnations of human evil, or to our hatred of Michael Milken during the junk bond scandals of the 1980s, or even to Bernie Madoff, who, while he may have invented a very effective kind of

Ponzi scheme, can certainly *not* be credited with inventing, as some would suggest, human greed or human evil.

Even in the face of rather unsavory characters like Tony Hayward, and tragic situations like the current massive oil spill, it might be good to remind ourselves that, within each of us, there is at least a little Tony Hayward, a little Bernie Madoff, a little Michael Milken, and, God only knows, maybe even a little bit of Jack the Ripper. Feeling good about ourselves, indeed, is a very wonderful thing, particularly when those feelings are deserved. But all too often, I suspect, it comes at the price of feeling sometimes unjustly and inhumanly bad about others, who, like all of us in times of trouble, and in the immortal words of now-vilified Tony Hayward, "want to get their lives back."

Which is a very human thing to want, even for a villain.

June, 2010

CHANGE WE DON'T BELIEVE IN

American culture, as President Obama recently and accurately put it to Peter Baker of the *New York Times*, is "not a culture that's built on patience." We no longer live for the centuries, or the decades, but by the nanoseconds and pixels. We complain when our internet server doesn't serve up its secrets quickly enough, or when our ATMs take more than a second to produce cash. So it's logical, as well, that we aren't terribly patient with our politics . . . or our politicians: The change they ask us to believe in is interpreted as an *immediate* change, the cures for our ills as *instant* cures, quick as a Google search, painless as Novocain.

This, too, has been the fate of our current President. Having inherited the results of eight years of arguably the worst administration in American history, he must now wrestle with the impatience of an electorate that expects him, in hardly twenty-one months, to have ended two wars, cured the worst recession since the Great Depression, and passed a reform of health care that no fewer than eleven American presidents have failed to achieve.

"Patience," former British Prime Minister and novelist Benjamin Disraeli once said, "is a necessary ingredient of genius." Even poets, hardly famed for their political acumen, have had more intelligent things to say about our present predicament than our impatient electorate. What every sane public needs, intoned the English poet Tennyson, is not only "some reverence for the laws ourselves have made," but also "some *patient* force to change them when we will."

But, here across the ocean from our former colonial power, "change" is a word we Americans love to hear—and will vote for at the drop of a hat—while "patience" is something we consider the monopoly of snails and chess players.

"How poor are they that have not patience! What wound did ever heal but by degrees?" asks Iago in Shakespeare's *Othello*, a question not easily answered by phrases such as "Yes we can." In retrospect, a far more honest slogan for the Obama campaign might have been "Yes we can . . . but slowly," a motto that would have gotten the candidate about as far as admitting he would raise taxes got Walter Mondale in 1984.

The fact is, however, that we Americans resist like poison the undeniable truth of the human condition: that true and meaningful change is *always* slow and painful, and requires a great deal of the very introspection and agitation both the media and the public denigrate as "waffling."

Yet it is only when we are finally mature enough as a

nation to elect a President and a Congress who not only promise us change, but demand of us patience, that we will finally have reached our national adulthood . . .

Unfortunately, however, I don't think I'm patient enough to wait for that.

September, 2010

TAKING BACK
THE SADDLE

"Things," wrote our greatest American philosopher, Ralph Waldo Emerson some one hundred fifty years ago, "are in the saddle, and ride mankind." I think of Emerson more and more these days, at this season in particular, when the mad consumer frenzy—the thing that is supposed to bring our moribund economy, and, with it, our moribund selves, back to life—is at a fever pitch, and we are bombarded with commercials for iPods and iPads, MP3 players and Blackberries, Kindles and MacBooks, but very few, if any, *real* books at all.

All of these, we are told, will not just improve the economy: they will improve our lives.

Though the former, undoubtedly, is true, at least in the short run, I very much doubt, indeed, I'd give odds against, the second. For "it's the things things stand for that make us mute," as I myself wrote in a poem some twenty-five years ago, and the deeper hunger that lies behind our hunger for objects, and the greed of those who feed it is, alas, nothing those objects can cure, or even begin to heal.

It is not merely a nation that has an economy, we might remind ourselves this season, but the soul, and one of the primary definitions of the word economy itself is that it is "efficiency and conservation of effort in the operation or achievement of something." So it might, prudently, be good to know *what* it is we are trying to achieve.

Here is just a brief list of the wounds I believe our hunger for objects tries to conceal: loneliness, spiritual hunger, love-lessness, alienation from nature, and—just in case those aren't enough—a lack of any sense of permanence and community, all of which leave us and the marketers who chase us from store to store in search of bargains without a center from which to resist.

"The ceremony of innocence is drowned," wrote the great Irish poet Yeats, "The best lack all conviction, while the worst / Are full of passionate intensity." It's the very same "passionate intensity," I would suggest as we commence this season of conspicuous consumption, that fuels all too much of our shopping, the perverse suggestion that what our MasterCards can buy is "priceless," while what our hearts truly yearn for can be easily obtained.

The truth, however, as anyone clear-headed enough to put down their screens and keyboards for a moment and look into their hearts will readily see, is that shopping is not a cure, but an anesthetic, that technology ought to be our servant *not* our subject, that the gifts most of us truly long for cannot be purchased at Walmart or T.J.Maxx, or even at Gabe's, but must be paid for in the more-difficult-to-convey and yet more readily available currency of the human heart.

This Christmas, as in most years, thousands of families will sit around the house watching *A Christmas Carol* and *It's a Wonderful Life*, many of them on the newly-purchased flat screen TVs and iPads whose very existence flies in the face of the values those timeless films seek to convey.

Sentimental though it may seem, what I would suggest instead—not on some Black Friday or Cyber Monday, but on some purely human Tuesday or Wednesday—is to click the "off" button on your remotes, gaze into the face, rather than the Facebook, of someone you love or the tree outside your window, lift a glass of eggnog into the air and remind yourselves of what we are when the modem goes bad and the internet turns off, when the power is down and all that is left to light our way is what the poet Howard Nemerov called "the rarely tinseled treasures of the world," seen through the sometimes dim—but nonetheless unextinguishable—power of the human heart.

December, 2010

RIGHT TO
BEAR HARMS

Among the many pieties spouted since the shooting of Congresswoman Gabrielle Giffords and the killing of six innocent people in Tucson, most remarkable of all has been the virtual absence of a certain word from most of the commentaries: *guns*. The heated political rhetoric, the decrease in civility in our public life, and the Tea Party have all been blamed for the tragedy, but very little has been said about the *weapon* that was used for the Arizona shootings, as well as those at Virginia Tech and Columbine and countless assassinations, including John and Robert Kennedy, Martin Luther King, Malcolm X, and Mahatma Gandhi—namely, the gun.

"If guns are outlawed," an NRA slogan of the 1970s went, "only outlaws will have guns." "Guns don't kill people," goes a more recent update, "people kill people." But it hardly takes a pundit's intelligence to realize the vapidity of such sayings: The fact is that outlaws, along with many law-abiding citizens, *do* have guns, and that it is people *with* guns—*not* with bows and arrows—who kill people.

Since Senator Joe Manchin has just wrapped up his "Common Sense Tour" of West Virginia, I'd like to offer him a bit of common sense. For one, I would suggest it doesn't require a literary mind to realize that it is no great metaphorical leap from a senatorial candidate firing a rifle through the Cap and Trade Bill to that of a mentally fragile twenty-two-year-old firing a pistol through the head of a Congresswoman. Secondly, I would remind him *and* President Obama, whom I otherwise admire—and other politicians who lack the political courage to state the obvious—of a few salient facts:

1. There are roughly 300 million firearms owned by civilians in the United States, roughly 100 million of which are handguns.

2. Between 40 and 45 percent of all households own guns and roughly 68 percent of all murders are committed using them.

3. Guns make it significantly easier for would-be killers to act out their murderous impulses, since they allow them to kill from afar, maintain a greater element of surprise and anonymity, kill larger and stronger people than themselves, and murder crowds of people at once.

Despite all this, a Gallup poll conducted in October revealed that only 44 percent of Americans said laws governing sales of firearms should be made stricter. What this means, in effect, is that only politicians who are independent and courageous enough to go *against* public opinion and seek to educate, rather than merely respond to, voters will be able to help reverse our current murderous trend.

As for myself, I would be more than happy to see my taxes increased to pay for federally financed archery lessons for our present and prospective hunters and target shooters. That way, at least, I can feel secure in the knowledge that what they have in their sights and those I carry in my heart, in all likelihood, won't be the same.

As for Representative Giffords, who not long ago boasted that she herself owned a Glock 9 millimeter handgun and was a pretty good shot, I suspect that, were she able to speak now at all, she might say the very same thing.

January, 2011

THE DIRTIEST
WORD IN AMERICA

As any contemporary politician who survives an election knows, there is no dirtier word in American politics than *taxes*. The way to get elected to virtually any office in the country these days seems to be by voicing platitudes about "getting government off our backs" and being taxed to death, though the reality is that we are among the *least* taxed, and the least besieged by government, of all industrialized democracies. New Hampshire, a state that has long prided itself on having neither a sales nor an income tax, also proudly proclaims on its state license plates that its citizens must "live free or die," a saying I myself have come to interpret more precisely as "live *for* free, or else leave."

But "nothing," as our greatest American philosopher, Ralph Waldo Emerson proclaimed some 150 years ago, "is free," including life in a civilized society itself, and the more quickly we embrace that fact the more quickly we may have both a humane and responsible government and an enlightened citizenry with which to elect it. More than twenty years ago, the first George Bush asked us to read his lips, and then, in a near-scream that actually required no lip-reading at all, proclaimed "No new taxes!" a pledge he was quick to renege on when even he came to realize that no taxes meant, in essence, no government.

But we Americans, who like living on credit so much that we have virtually mortgaged our children's futures to pay for it, like to think of taxes, to paraphrase Thomas Paine, as something that at first was plunder and later assumed the softer name of revenue. What we forget, however, amidst all the political demagoguery about taxes is that, as Chief Justice Holmes put it in his opinion in the 1904 Supreme Court case of *Compañia de Tabacos v. Collector*, "taxes are what we pay for civilized society." Taxes are what we pay in order to have roads, schools, fire departments, police, and— in more humane societies than ours—universal health care and free public universities. As Plato put it in *The Republic*: "Where there is an income tax, the just man will pay more and the unjust less on the same amount of income."

My friends in Scandinavia and Europe—many of whom pay as much as sixty percent or more of their income in taxes, are *happy* to pay those taxes, and for one simple reason: They feel, as any good bargainer would, that they are getting their money's worth. Yet here in the land of the free it has therefore long baffled me that the very same people who seem to think nothing of paying thousands of dollars in memberships to their various country clubs for the privilege of gently groomed golf courses and well-maintained tennis courts apparently feel that taxing them to pay for roads, schools, national defense and—God forbid!—a safety net for the less fortunate among us is the equivalent of some sort of financial form of capital punishment.

The fact is, I *like* paying taxes—though I would like it a helluva lot better if the rich were paying their fare share as well. Running against taxes, it seems to me, is like running against democracy itself, and overlooking the conventional yet rather profound wisdom that what the government gives it must first take away. Our taxes, after all, as President Franklin Roosevelt once said, are the dues that we pay for the privileges of membership in an organized society. And, like with any club, it seems to me, you don't deserve to be a member if you don't want to pay your dues.

January, 2011

GAY MARRIAGE AND
THE PURSUIT OF HAPPINESS

Among the "unalienable Rights" guaranteed to us by the Declaration of Independence, as virtually everyone knows, is "the pursuit of Happiness," a right most Americans, for their own good, support. But, lately in our increasingly extreme and divided country, more and more of us seem to feel that the happiness others are free to pursue should be defined by *us*: They have, in other words, the right to be happy, just as long as *their* happiness doesn't collide with *our* values.

Take, for example, the suddenly front-and-center issue of gay marriage, and, strangely enough, the pursuit of happiness doesn't seem all it's cracked up to be. Marriage, for many Americans, seems to be the kind of happiness that is only to be pursued by heterosexuals, preferably of the Christian faith.

Now, I have a son myself, who, though he is not quite yet of a fully marriageable age, is quickly getting there, and I must confess to a kind of narcissistic hope that he will, indeed, eventually marry a woman, not a man, and bear one or two biological grandchildren for his aging parents. But what if that isn't the kind of happiness he chooses to pursue? What if he turns out to be gay? Or, worse yet in most eyes, to become transgendered, and live out his days as a woman? Will I then suddenly rescind the Declaration of Independence which it is every human being's right once emancipated from those who fathered and mothered them? Will I seek to deny him the happiness *he* has chosen for the sake of the happiness that fulfills my own narcissistic fantasies and dreams?

I certainly hope not, and—in a moment of somewhat self-congratulation—I don't think I will. For the simple reason that it is *his* happiness he is entitled to pursue, not mine.

And so it is with gay marriage, and our President's and Vice-President's commendable, and I believe sincere, embrace of them. There is no culture on this earth, to my knowledge, that hasn't known homosexuality, whether condoned or condemned, in some form, and it seems to me both morally and psychologically dubious that any of us have the right to deny to those so disposed, or destined, their own fair slice of the universal happiness pie.

"Whenever the people are for gay marriage or medical marijuana or assisted suicide," political commentator Bill Maher has observed, "suddenly the 'will of the people' goes out the window." And so, indeed, it is: The same people who are Libertarians or Tea Partiers when it comes to abolishing Social Security or opposing universal health care, are suddenly wild about government when it comes to opposing gay marriage.

Though I have long made my living in a profession where metaphor and symbolism hold great weight, when it comes to the pursuit of happiness, I'm a literalist: The right to that pursuit is exactly what it says it is: *a right*—up to the point, of course, where you can do genuine, rather than imaginary, harm to someone else.

Should my son fall in love with and marry a man, or decide to change his sex, or—as he has already done—join a military I myself never wanted anything to do with, good for him. As he once, while still a teenager, said to me when, after separating from his mother, I asked him if he liked the woman I was going out with at the time:

"Dad," he replied, "as long as you're happy."

February, 2013

THE SWEETEST DREAM
THAT LABOR KNOWS

"The fact," wrote poet Robert Frost in his 1915 poem *Mowing*, "is the sweetest dream that labor knows," a thought which seems entirely lost on the American public these days. We seem collectively to think, instead, that *opinions* are the sweetest dream labor knows, and that everyone who has one is somehow entitled to equal time in print and on our airwaves in which to express it. For every Paul Krugman, we are told, there must be a Glenn Beck, for every Jon Stewart a George Will, for every Joe Biden a Sarah Palin, for every Republican moderate a Donald Trump.

But there's something wrong with this theory. It confuses the commendable belief that democracy demands we listen to diverse *interpretations* of fact with the fallacy that all such so-called interpretations are equal. But "facts," as our second President, John Adams, pointed out, "are stubborn things, and whatever may be our wishes, our inclinations, or the dictates of our passions, they cannot alter the state of evidence." A fact is something that is *true* about a subject and can be tested or proven. An opinion is what someone *thinks* about that subject, frequently introduced by words such as *"I believe . . . ," "It's obvious . . . ," or "They should . . ."* Facts are the province of juries to determine; opinions are the work of judges to craft.

It's forty-four degrees and rainy in Morgantown as I write this. *Those* are facts. But whether those facts render it beautiful, or inclement, weather is—no matter what the statistics—a matter of opinion. For my Mediterranean friends, this is the dead of winter; for myself, it's a harbinger of spring. Facts have an objective reality. Opinions don't.

Here are some other indisputable facts: Genetic engineering is now a fact. That Chaucer was a real person is an undisputed fact as well. The top two percent of wealthy Americans now earn over forty percent of our national income; almost ten percent of young African American men are behind bars; the U.S. national debt is now some $14.3 trillion, or roughly $46,000 per citizen. Whatever one thinks may be *responsible* for this latter group of facts and what we ought to *do* about them are matters of opinion; but the facts themselves are what they are: objectively verifiable and indisputably the case.

I doubt that anyone who is truly serious about democracy, or about the media's obligations within it, would want to suggest that alternative facts should always be granted equal time. Are we, for example, obligated to provide equal time to Holocaust deniers? To those, like Donald Trump, who believe that President Obama is not an American-born citizen? To those who, despite all the evidence to the contrary, still argue that women are inferior to men, or homosexuality a disease?

"People in old times had convictions," wrote the great German poet Heinrich Heine. "We moderns only have opinions." But "a little fact," as Ralph Waldo Emerson pointed out, "is worth a whole limbo of dreams."

Most of what I've just said here, of course—and don't let anyone tell you otherwise—is purely a matter of opinion.

And that, dear listeners, is most indisputably a fact.

May, 2012

HEROES WITH A THOUSAND FACES

America, in case you haven't noticed, is drowning in heroes. Almost every day, new ones are anointed by the media, from Captain "Sully" Sullenberger, who successfully landed US Airways Flight 1549 in the Hudson in 2009, to the members of Navy Seal Team 6 that killed Osama Bin Laden in Pakistan last week. Just as there hardly seems to be a book around these days that *hasn't* won a prize, the type of human being that hasn't been declared a hero, too, is an endangered species.

I had a hero as a child—a German-born physician by the name of Albert Schweitzer. Along with being one of the world's greatest living organists, Schweitzer wrote several other books on music and religion and, as if that wasn't enough, devoted most of his adult life to work as a medical missionary in French Equatorial Africa. He was awarded the Nobel Peace Prize in 1953, and died in 1965, when I was fifteen.

Being a mere pre-adolescent at the time, I couldn't have articulated what I thought a hero was. But—like Supreme Court Potter Stewart speaking of pornography in 1964—I knew one when I saw one. The word "hero" is derived from the Ancient Greek word for "demi-god" and came, over the centuries, to refer to characters who, in the face of danger and adversity, displayed courage and self sacrifice for the greater good of humanity. "A hero," as mythologist Joseph Campbell put it, "is someone who has given his or her life to something bigger than oneself." A good definition, methinks, the kind that might endure over time.

Several members of my family were brutally exterminated by Hitler during the Holocaust. Yet the sight of Adolf Eichmann hanging from a rope in Jerusalem in 1963 provided me no great joy. Nor did I consider his executioner a hero. A competent and well-trained hangman, that's for sure, but, as far as I was concerned, no hero. Eichmann's hanging didn't undo the tragedies he perpetrated: It merely deepened them.

As an American and a citizen of this world, I'm certainly glad that Bin Laden no longer exists as a threat to the innocent. But we also need to remind ourselves that he, too, was once an innocent child like our own children and ourselves, howsoever difficult that may be to believe, and, at his death, was composed, as the poet Auden put it, "of eros and of dust," and of the same roughly six quarts of blood and 108 bones as the rest of us.

As a member of that same species myself, I am far more interested in how, and why, there are Bin Ladens in this world, and how to prevent more of them from developing, than I am in seeing any photograph of his corpse. And whoever might explain *that* to me, I'm convinced, would be even more deserving of the name hero than those who removed him from our further consideration.

May, 2011

A MODEST PROPOSAL

It's the silly season, as I call it, when a bunch of people all of whom want to be President—but none of whom seem to want, or believe in, anything else—heave their slogans and one-liners at the lowest common denominator of our national intelligence. They try to convince us that what they demonize as ObamaCare isn't really health care, that the job they are vying for is better suited to a salesman than a statesman.

Statesmanship, for that matter, seems to be a thing of the past. "A politician," wrote the theologian James Freeman Clarke "thinks of the next election. A statesman, of the next generation." Our current politicians can't seem to think past the next debate.

On the night of March 31st, 1968, a certain American president provided an example of the lost art of statesmanship, when he spoke the following words:

I do not believe that I should devote an hour or a day of my time to any personal partisan causes or to any duties other than the awesome duties of this office—the Presidency of your country.

That president was Lyndon Johnson, speaking at the height of the Vietnam War, a speech that famously ended with the words "I shall not seek, and I will not accept, the nomination of my party for another term as your President."

Whatever one might think of Johnson's motives, the sentiments his words expressed were not so much political as they were statesman-like. For "a statesman," as former French President Pompidou once commented, "is a politician who places himself at the service of the nation. A politician is a statesman who places the nation at his service."

So now may be high time for at least a few of the Republican presidential candidates—many of whom are prime examples of Adlai Stevenson's theory that "a politician is a statesman who approaches every question with an open mouth"—to close theirs and place themselves in the nation's service instead. Instead of seeking to outdo the Democrats in the Machiavellian machinations of contemporary politics, a true Republican patriot might seek to follow Johnson's example and, to put it bluntly, bow out.

"In the interests of my country's well-being," he or she might say, "I am herewith suspending my campaign for President of the United States. While I may not agree with all of this President's policies, I wholeheartedly support his wish to unite our nation and find a way out of our present difficulties. In the interests of that shared enterprise, I wish to stand for the proposition that I hold the welfare of this nation above the concerns of my party or my own political career."

Such a politician, at this time in our history, might be a figure worthy of both our trust and our admiration, perhaps even a statesman. He or she might even—by declaring themselves less interested in their own fate than in the fate of their nation—deserve to be President.

September, 2011

ENCORE!

The first intelligible word my son ever spoke, in a tiny restaurant in the South of France and over what was obviously a delicious slice of apple tart, was the word *encore!*, which means *more* in French. I see now, though I didn't realize it then, that my infant son possessed a kind of prescience concerning the human condition: We are, indeed, the species that perpetually wants— and has almost always gotten—more.

"You never know what is enough," wrote the poet William Blake, "unless you know what is *more* than enough." But *enough*, unlike *more*, is a word we Americans aren't terribly fond of, and the politics of the moment, and of the conceivable future, reflects that state of mind. Consequently, the pandering of our politicians, and the lack of realism of the policies they support, depends on a very different definition of happiness.

While, over the past fifty or so years, we have constantly demanded more, it seems incontestable that, in the coming years, we will have to settle for less. Ironically enough, almost all the research also suggests that, during our years of plenty, we have grown more and more depressed. A recent analysis of the World Database of Happiness covering the years 1946 to 2006, found rising happiness levels in nineteen of twenty-six countries around the world—but the United States was *not* among them.

But how can this be? Shouldn't more money, more possessions, more opportunity, more choices, and more leisure, also lead to *more* happiness? Why—with the entire Western world joining my once-infant son in chanting *encore!*—do we seem ever more miserable? And how, with many of the things we are in demand of (like oil, natural resources, arable land, and the bounties of the sea) rapidly diminishing, can we go on saying *more* and have our lives make sense?

The cure for our present economic ills, we are told, lies in remaining true to my son's spirit—more demand, more goods, more consumption, more technology, and with them, logically enough, more jobs, and, consequently, more prosperity. This makes a certain economic sense, but only in the short term . . . and only, I would suggest, at a great human cost. For, while the clamor for *more* may well grow the economy, there's strong evidence to suggest that the spirit of *enough* may nourish the spirit. If wisdom, rather than expediency, guided our politics, it would foster such a spirit of enough for those who have so much, and more for those who have so little.

"My friends and I have been coddled long enough by a billionaire-friendly Congress," Warren Buffett wrote recently in *The New York Times.* "It's time for our government to get serious about shared sacrifice." But getting serious about shared sacrifice also entails, for some of us, at least, being able to say "enough." Or, as I would say of myself right now, *more* than enough. Until more of us, as a people, are able to say that, I doubt that the gods of happiness will be willing to listen to our far less urgent, and somehow child-like, demand that is always crying out: *encore!*

October, 2011

LYNCHED

The last public hanging in the United States, or so we'd like to think, took place on August 14th, 1936, when an estimated crowd of 20,000 people thronged Owensboro, Kentucky, to watch a twenty-seven-year-old black man by the name of Rainey Bethea be hanged for, among other crimes, the rape of a white woman.

While Bethea's sentencing bore the marks of racism and patriarchy that made purported black-on-white sexual crimes such fodder for lynch laws at the time, and the four-and-a-half-minute jury deliberation hardly had the look of solemnity, Bethea's actual guilt, at least, was fairly well established. He was granted, if nothing else, at least the dignity of a trial and a conviction.

Not so, however, for the following list of names—some of them ultimately tried and acquitted, others never (or not yet) tried, some simply falsely accused to begin with, and only two of whom were actually convicted: O. J. Simpson, the Duke lacrosse players, Richard Jewell, Amanda Knox,

Bernie Madoff, Michael Jackson's physician Conrad Murray, Dominique Strauss-Kahn, and, most recently, Jerry Sandusky (who, it turns out, was convicted and sentenced since this essay was written).

Jewell, you may remember, was the American security guard who became known in connection with the Centennial Olympic Park bombing at the 1996 Summer Olympics in Atlanta. Working as a security guard, he in fact discovered a pipe bomb, alerted police, and helped to evacuate the area before it exploded, saving many people from injury or potential death. Despite having never been charged, and later completely exonerated, he underwent a "trial by media," which took a lasting toll on his personal and professional life.

The fact is that the media in this country has introduced a new phenomenon into our criminal justice system: that of pre-trial, and pre-sentencing, public execution. Shackled and led from homes to police cars to courthouses and back again amid the flashing lights of the paparazzi, our celebrity suspects, investigated but not yet accused, accused but not yet tried, tried but not yet sentenced, are subjected to rituals of public humiliation and disgrace that make their ultimate sentences, should they ever arrive, benign by comparison.

Perhaps, it occurs to me, there is something primitive, almost primal, in our need for such public hangings and humiliations. Perhaps those ever-flashing flashbulbs are simply our contemporary version of the guillotine, the noose, the firing squad (they, too, after all, are "firing"), and the premature burial. The alleged crimes of the accused may be heinous indeed, but our inability to wait until the wheels of justice have their chance to turn is equally reprehensible . . . and may be even more damaging.

The literal texts of our Constitution and criminal justice system demand that individuals are innocent until proven guilty. But the realities of the human mind and our scandal-seeking imaginations more often suggest that where there's smoke, there's fire. What remains etched in our collective memory about these individuals are the accusations themselves, *not* their ultimate resolution. Convicted by flashbulbs and a fame-crazed public, the accused dangle before us, testimonies to the short distance we sometimes travel in the name of progress.

January, 2012

OF MINDS AND MINDFULNESS

A MIND OF WINTER

"One must have a mind of winter,"
the poet Wallace Stevens wrote,

> To regard the frost and the boughs
> Of the pine-trees crusted with snow;
>
> And have been cold a long time
> To behold the junipers shagged with ice,
> The spruces rough in the distant glitter
>
> Of the January sun; and not to think
> Of any misery in the sound of the wind.

Stevens, as he so often does, is speaking here mostly of death, a subject to which, it seems, our minds often tend to wander during this season. But, for me at least, winter is mostly about *life*—life, that is, at its most tranquil, its most peaceful, its most cozy, most romantic, and most familial. The view from winter's windows, for me, is not so much about the "Nothing that is not there and the nothing that is" with which Stevens' admittedly great poem ends, as about a particularly beautiful and consoling *something*—namely, snow.

"The hiss was now becoming a roar—the whole world was a vast moving screen of snow—but even now it said peace, it said remoteness, it said cold, it said sleep," Conrad Aiken writes in his much-anthologized 1932 story, *Silent Snow, Secret Snow.* And so, recently, it was here in Morgantown (and may well be again this New Year's Eve night), when a pre-Christmas snow blanketed the living and the dead in a glorious, immaculate dusting of white, rendering our already neighborly neighbors even *more* neighborly, calling a virtual halt to our cars and holding a starting gun up to our shovels, and calling forth recipes for split pea soup and hot mulled wine from our cookbooks, sweaters from our dresser drawers, and eliciting warm hands and bodies from those we love.

Freud considered the wish for homeostasis, for calm, for lack of passion and excitement, akin to what he called the death drive, or *thanatos.* But, for those of an already relatively calm and nesting disposition like myself, it's the life drive, or *eros,* that winter calls forth, making of beds a venue not only for sleep but for the consolations of the flesh, of kitchens a place not merely for nourishment, but for warmth, of the VCR and the television not merely places of retreat, but of repose.

"After all this, all this beautiful progress, the slow delicious advance of the postman through the silent and secret snow, the knock creeping closer each day, and the footsteps nearer, the audible compass of the world thus daily narrowed, narrowed, narrowed, as the snow soothingly and beautifully encroached and deepened," Aiken writes of his protagonist, a young boy named Paul Hasleman, and of his mysterious awareness of the "secret snow"' that signals his growing sense of detachment from the real world.

"You must choose between countries where you sweat, and countries where you think," Voltaire, obviously not a fan of hot weather, wrote, and I would tend to agree. The summer heat, much as I love the long daylight it brings with it, tends to deplete and enervate me; the winter cold brings not only my mind, but my body, to life. Is there anything more beautiful, for example, than stopping at a mid-slope ski lodge at noon, surrounded by the magnificent whiteness of snow, with one's face looking up into the winter sun? Is there any taste better than that of a warm meal and hot cup of coffee after a day on the cross-country trails at Cooper's Rock?

It's raining as I write this, but I'm the kind of person who tends to live in hope, rather than regret. Tonight, rumor has it, the rain will turn to snow, and tomorrow, if we're lucky and blessed, our next decade will begin with the world once more encased in white, the mind refreshed, the body filled with appetites and lusts, the slow and delicious advance of the postman approaching once more through the silent, secretive, and beautiful snow.

January, 2010

COLLEGE DAYS, DANGER DAYS

There was a time, not so long ago, when parents used to send their kids to college, not only so they could learn something, but with the consoling thought that college was a safe place, where minds and spirits could engage in their ruminations far from the battlefields of violence and the bedrooms of discord. But that era—not only according to my own son's reports from the field, but from reports I've gotten from all over the country—now seems part of a distant, somehow romantic, past.

A few months ago, my son, an honors freshman at the University of Virginia, called me, first, to report the murder of a father by his own son, a fellow honors scholar living in his dorm; then, a week or so later, to relate that a student had died, apparently of an alcohol overdose, after a local fraternity party. Then, just three or so weeks ago, he called to tell me of the brutal murder of twenty-two-year-old U.Va. senior and lacrosse player Yeardley Love by her former boyfriend, a U.Va. men's lacrosse star, just two weeks before her graduation.

All this took place only several months after, right here at West Virginia University, undergraduate Ryan Diviney was beaten nearly to death in front of a Dairy Mart store during an altercation over the profoundly significant subject of what team he happened to be rooting for in the World Series, and just a bit further in time from the murder of Yale doctoral student Annie Le in a building of Yale Medical School's Department of Pharmacology last September. Add to this three recent suicides at my own alma mater, Cornell, and what begins to emerge is a pretty disturbing picture of college life—*not* as the title of a seventies' film about college life, *A Small Circle of Friends*, but, rather, as an ever-widening circle of danger.

This is not to say that university life, at least in America, has ever entirely concerned itself exclusively with Plato and Aristotle, or Copernicus and Darwin. The life of the mind, at least in modern times, has always been accompanied by plenty of sex, drugs, and rock and roll—at least two of which, it might be argued, do little harm to the average post-adolescent's hormonal system. But sex, rock-and-roll, and hitting the books are no longer what college life seems about: *Now* there is also murder—sometimes, as in the Virginia Tech massacre, thirty-five in one fell swoop, sometimes in mere tragic integers of one—and, if not murder, rape, robbery, aggravated assault, then suicide.

My son, much to his mother's dismay, recently signed on to the National Guard, an act which led me to remark, only half-jokingly, that he may well be safer there than at college. Nonetheless, what the literature and the crime statistics show is that our college campuses, for the most part, remain safe places for students to study and live, with rates for all violent crime significantly lower than for the country at large. During the past decade, for example, there have been no fewer than 284 violent deaths on our college campuses, 130 of them as the result of shootings, 49 as the result of suicides, 34 of murder-suicides, and 41 of stabbings. With the exception of forcible rape, none of these statistics even approaches the percentages for the population at large. But, from where I sit as the parent of one of those students, that's 284 too many.

There are plenty of possible reasons for this phenomenon—the greater availability of firearms, the increase in the tension and anxiety of modern life, and the inability of colleges and universities to differentiate actual threats from the normal playing out of youthful romance and entanglement among them. But, although I've also been a therapist in a past life, I'm not here to analyze the causes: I'm just trying to describe the reality.

"Safety was the day's dull wisdom," is a line from a poem I wrote about my childhood, while a student myself, some thirty years ago. But all these recent events palpably remind me that worry about our children's safety may be more wise

than dull, and that the United Negro College Fund's sixty-five-year-old slogan—"A mind is a terrible thing to waste"—no longer holds true of the mind alone. What's even more frightening these days on our college campuses is the potential waste, not merely of minds, but of souls, cut short in the very institutions whose sacred mission it is to build them in the first place.

June, 2010

ON-LINE AND ON POINT, BUT WAY OFF COURSE

I did a rather radical thing the other day: I looked up various definitions of the word "education." "Education," went one, "is the process by which society deliberately transmits its accumulated knowledge, skills, and values from one generation to another." Then I did something else. I googled the words "on-line education" and came up with a staggering 698,000,000 hits. I then googled "traditional education" and got 17,000,000, about one fortieth that number. "Liberal education" elicited a paltry 7,180,000.

All this has done something to confirm a suspicion I've long had: that, unless we become very vigilant very soon, education as we have known it for hundreds of years will shortly come to an end. What we will have instead, what we, in fact, are having already, is a virtual tsunami of websites, videos, power points, emails, and visual applications in whose wake the two most crucial aspects of education—human interaction and human thought—are virtually being swept away.

For years now an increasing percentage of the so-called "lectures" I've attended by academic colleagues—gratefully, very few of them here at WVU—have consisted more and more of their reading to an audience from Power Point presentations and showing video clips than of actually speaking. The lecture has thus slowly moved from the experience of watching and hearing someone *think* out loud to listening to them *read* out loud, from being *inspired* to being *entertained*.

The truth is that, from the point of view of genuine learning, on-line education is an oxymoron, whose bottom line isn't education, but cost. On-line and multi-media education, to be sure, have their purpose, and their place. They can prove a godsend for the disabled and infirm, an oasis in the educational desert of the aged and geographically isolated. But, like saccharin for sugar, or tofu for beef, they are merely a substitute, not a replacement, and it's a travesty of truth to advertise them as anything else.

As the eminent environmental educator David Orr pointed out in a 1990 address, the *way* in which our learning occurs is at least as important as the content of any particular courses. That's because education is not simply a matter of content, but of contact, not merely a matter of conveying information, but of soul and sensibility.

The great teachers I have had in my life have taught me, not merely by presenting *information*, but by conveying their spiritual and intellectual *presence*, by allowing me to interact with, not merely their mouths in motion, but their minds at play. They conveyed to me not merely the fact that they could read, but that they could think, not merely that they could answer, but that they could respond, not merely that they could entertain, but inspire. Those are qualities no website, no power point, no email has ever been able to communicate . . . nor ever will.

Real education, and here's another possible definition, takes place when two or more intelligences illuminate each other . . . *not* two screens. It has been taking place at least since the first human being ever uttered the words "Do you know?" and relies for what it is on human speech, human presence, and human eye contact. None of which, gratefully, a computer screen or a pointer will ever replace. Nor ever should.

April, 2011

NONE OF
YOUR BUSINESS

Now that all you out there listening have sent off your Hallmark Cards, delivered your flowers, and UPSed your chocolates to your various beloveds, I can feel safe to say it: I *detest*, have *always* detested, Valentine's Day.

The Europeans, it is said, once believed that, on February 14th, the birds begin to choose their mates. But my own belief, no matter what the birds may do, is that each February 14th we humans engage in the falsest, most emotionally unreliable, behavior of our lives. And at least some of my fellow humans seem to agree: A recent Reuters survey of 24,000 people in 23 countries found that 21 percent of adults would rather spend February 14th with their pet than their spouse.

So, how do I hate Valentine's Day? Let me count the ways:

One. Valentine's Day, as I see it, is the New Year's Eve of the heart. Just as we are so fervently implored to "have fun" the night of December 31st that it is almost impossible truly to have it, love—being the hardest of all emotions to feel on demand—is about as likely to be experienced on the 14th of February as snow in Phoenix in August. But feel it, we are told, we nonetheless must.

Two. Valentine's Day, along with being the day of more false and unspontaneous feeling than any other, is also the day of more sentimentalized and foolish consumerism. While, no doubt, a blessing for Hallmark, Godiva, and Teleflora, it's a curse on the pocketbooks of the poor, beleaguered, already over-consuming masses who feel compelled to "say it with flowers" or some other herd-validated mark of sincerity when what they would truly prefer is simply save their sheckels and shut up.

A noble example of this can be found in the life of a friend of mine, a highly reasonable, intelligently irreverent philosopher, who, when a boyfriend of hers summoned a singing trio of men in red pajamas, starting off with a chorus of *"Zippedee Doo Da,"* to her university office on Valentine's Day some years ago, immediately realized this wasn't the man for her and ended the relationship.

Three. As further evidence of this, even as I type these very words, a message entitled "Shopping online for your Valentine" appears in my email box. "Dear Michael C Blumenthal," it begins:

Looking for the perfect Valentine's Day gift? You'll find the best selection of gifts, like a Nordstrom gift card or an iPod nano, at Mileage Plus Mall. Plus, as a first-time Mileage Plus Mall shopper, you'll earn *500 bonus miles* when you spend $50 by February 14th, 2010. Isn't that a deal to love?

Well, frankly, *no*, it's *not* a deal to love, or even give a damn about, at least for me. What I would *truly* love instead is to be left alone by the telemarketers, internet advertisers, disseminators of heart-shaped pink objects, and all the rest, and be allowed to express my sentiments when, and if, I feel like it . . . not according to the artificially inseminated demands of some merely calendrical muse.

"The creative mind," the psychologist Carl Gustav Jung wisely said, "*plays* with the objects it loves." What I take Jung to mean is that such a mind feels obligated to convey sincerity, *not* chocolates and Hallmark cards. In fact, my message to my Valentine, whoever she may be, echoes the words of the great German poet Goethe, who, it seems to me, hit the nail of love—and the true spirit of Valentine's Day—squarely on the head. "*If I love you,*" he wrote, and I echo his sentiments here, "*what business is it of yours.*"

February, 2012

IN PRAISE OF
DOING NOTHING

I've spent much of this summer doing something only the privileged, the tenured, and those not hankering for a promotion in the first place get to do: namely, *nothing*. Now, I use the word nothing advisedly—a bit like the poet Wallace Stevens did when he spoke of "Nothing that is not there and the nothing that is."

The fact is, I feel like I've done quite a bit of something, staring into space in my Hungarian garden, listening to the music of Schumann and Locatelli and, evenings, to jazz, thinking about life and its many ups and downs, working on my Hungarian cooking.

In fact, this has seemed to me like one of the more productive summers I've had in a long time, but what do I have to show for it?—Nothing . . . sort of. No book manuscripts, no new articles, a mere handful of poems, a few good books read. Beyond that, nothing.

"They toil not, neither do they spin," goes the epigraph from the Book of Matthew to the poet John Keats' famous

"Ode to Indolence." And I think it's fair to say that, at least this summer, I didn't toil much, nor did I spin. In an 1819 letter to his brother and sister-in-law George and Georgiana about the poem, Keats described his indolence this way: "This is the only happiness; and is a rare instance of advantage in the body overpowering the Mind," and then, in the poem itself, described it like this:

> Was it a silent deep-disguised plot
> To steal away, and leave without a task
> My idle days? Ripe was the drowsy hour;
> The blissful cloud of summer-indolence
> Benumb'd my eyes; my pulse grew less and less.

We live in a world that relentlessly requires tangible accomplishments, lines to be added to one's resumé and impress others with at cocktail parties. Our culture values restlessness of the mind over the natural indolence of the body, which—at least if it's *my* body—loves nothing more than to sit in a comfortable chair, staring out at the world. Even freewheeling Bob Dylan, in his 1967 song *Too Much of Nothing*, counseled that "Too much of nothing / Can make a man ill at ease." *What I Did On My Summer Vacation*, after all, was the title of one of the first essays virtually all of us wrote in elementary school. *Nothing* would surely have received a failing grade.

Nonetheless, I would argue that I'm a better, and wiser, person for all the nothing I did this summer . . . I feel more at peace, more at home in my own body . . . benevolently less accomplished. I may not have added any lines to my resumé, but I feel that I've added several years to my life . . . if not quantitatively, than at least qualitatively.

I have, no doubt, done little to enhance my status on the job market—which, gratefully, I don't find myself on—and probably even less to enhance it on the meat market . . . a market I'm, gratefully, also no longer a part of. Instead, I'm spent some weeks that remind me of a stanza from my old friend W. D. Snodgrass's marvelous poem, "April Inventory":

> The green catalpa tree has turned
> All white; the cherry blooms once more.
> In one whole year I haven't learned
> A blessed thing they pay you for.
> The blossoms snow down in my hair;
> The trees and I will soon be bare.

Indeed, the trees will soon be bare, but, for now at least, they are still in bloom, and so am I, with all that nothing I have accumulated for myself in the name of what I consider more important, and more enduring.

August, 2012

ABOUT THE AUTHOR

Michael Blumenthal, presently Visiting Professor of Law and Co-Director of the Immigration Clinic at West Virginia University College of Law, is the author of eight books of poetry, most recently *No Hurry: Poems 2000–2012.*

A graduate of Cornell Law School and formerly Director of Creative Writing at Harvard, he is also the author of the memoir *All My Mothers and Fathers.* His novel *Weinstock Among The Dying,* which won *Hadassah Magazine's* Harold U. Ribelow Prize for the best work of Jewish fiction, has just been re-issued in paperback, and his collection of essays from Central Europe, *When History Enters the House,* was published in 1998.

A frequent translator from German, French, and Hungarian and former psychotherapist, he spent a month in South Africa in May 2007 working with orphaned infant chacma baboons at the C.A.R.E. foundation, an experience about which he has written for *Natural History* and *The*

Washington Post Magazine. His book-length account of this experience, *"Because They Needed Me": The Incredible Struggle of Rita Miljo To Save The Baboons of South Africa,* was published in Germany in 2012 and featured at the Frankfurt Book Fair in the fall of that year, and will be published in the U.S. in 2014.

His first collection of short stories, *The Greatest Jewish-American Lover in Hungarian History,* is also forthcoming in 2014 from the Etruscan Press.